Treasures

*Reflections and prayers
on favourite Bible passages*

Nick Fawcett

First published in 2004 by

KEVIN MAYHEW LTD

Buxhall, Stowmarket, Suffolk, IP14 3BW

E-mail: info@kevinmayhewltd.com

KINGSGATE PUBLISHING INC

1000 Pannell Street, Suite G, Columbia, MO 65201

E-mail: sales@kingsgatepublishing.com

The material in this book first appeared in *Daily Prayer*
and *The Fawcett Bible Studies*.

9 8 7 6 5 4 3 2 1 0

ISBN 1 84417 264 3

Catalogue No. 1500706

Cover design by Angela Selfe

Edited by Katherine Laidler

Typesetting by Fiona Connell-Finch

Printed and bound in Great Britain

Contents

Introduction

Some passages of the Bible stand out in the memory, don't they? While the whole of Scripture is important, neglected at our peril, certain verses capture our imagination or speak to us in a way that few others can begin to. Who can forget the words of the 23rd Psalm, the parables of Jesus, or the wonderful teaching of Paul in 1 Corinthians 13 on the gift of love? These are just some of the countless passages to have encouraged, comforted, strengthened and inspired Christians across the centuries.

We must, of course, beware of being too selective when it comes to reading the Bible, or we will end up avoiding whatever might challenge our particular viewpoint, thus effectively closing our ears to anything that God might wish to say to us. He has an uncanny knack of speaking through the most unlikely of verses, stretching our horizons and disturbing the comfortable status quo. On the other hand, well-loved verses can remind us of the underlying realities of the gospel, offering reassurance in times of doubt, support in times of challenge and hope in times of despair. Some, indeed, become so familiar to us that they seem almost like old friends. We may even know them off by heart, yet their power to challenge, inspire and encourage remains undiminished, God continuing to speak through them in new and wonderful ways.

In this short compilation I have drawn upon my book *Daily Prayer* and various volumes of my Bible Study series to offer brief reflections on 15 unforgettable passages from the Gospels, each supplemented by a simple closing prayer. The selection is inevitably a personal one, but I suspect many of the passages I have chosen will also feature among your own personal favourites. It is my hope that they will speak as powerfully to you as they have to me.

NICK FAWCETT

Matthew 5:9

Blessed are the peacemakers

Blessed are the peacemakers,
for God will call them his children.

Reflection

A year or so ago an astonishingly moving story hit the headlines. It was just a few days after a suicide bomber at an Israeli wedding reception had left several people dead and countless others maimed and injured – men, women and children, one moment enjoying a family celebration and the next caught up in the most unspeakable carnage. Few incidents summed up more tragically the depth of hatred between Jew and Arab, the level of atrocities on both sides seeming to know no bounds. The story I have in mind, though, was very different. It concerned the father of a young man killed in an accident. Distraught with grief though he was, he agreed to donate his son's organs to a hospitalised patient in urgent need of a transplant. Nothing extraordinary about that, you might think, except that the donor was an Arab and the patient an Israeli! 'I wanted my son's death to bring life,' explained the father, 'whether it be to Jew or Arab.' The contrast could hardly be more poignant nor the example more challenging. A small act but a massive gesture that, for a few hours at least, spoke of peace and reconciliation.

Would we have acted the same in that man's place? I wonder. Our situation may be far removed from his, but in innumerable ways we have the opportunity every day either to act as peacemakers or to perpetuate the things that cause division. We can show forgiveness or nurse grievances, swallow our pride or thrust ourselves forward, admit mistakes or refuse to bend, make the first move to heal wounds or resist every olive branch. All of us in our daily relationships can work for harmony and reconciliation, but few of us take the opportunity as often as we should. Which are we: peacemakers or peace-breakers?

Prayer

Loving God,
    forgive all within me that makes for conflict –
    my pride, greed, envy and intolerance,
    my nursing of grievances and unwillingness to forgive.
Teach me to heal wounds rather than create them,
    to see what unites rather than what divides,
    to work for peace in whatever ways I can.
May the peace I so often pray for begin here and now
    with me,
    through Jesus Christ my Lord.
Amen.

Matthew 6:19-21

Treasure in heaven

Do not amass earthly treasures, vulnerable to attack by moths, rust or thieves breaking in and making off with them. Instead accrue treasures in heaven, susceptible to neither moths, rust or theft. For you can be sure of this: wherever your treasure is to be found, your heart will be found there too.

Reflection

Money we are told, can't buy us happiness. Do you believe that? Probably most of us will nod our heads sagely as if to say, 'How true!' but if put to the test, few of us would turn our backs on a fortune, or even a small bonus, were we to be offered it – I know I wouldn't.

It may not be able to guarantee happiness but there's no doubt that having enough to pay your way helps prevent much that can cause unhappiness. Yet the fact remains that the most important things in life are beyond price: things like friendship, health, self-esteem, motivation, peace of mind, fulfilment. Some of these, indeed, may be lost rather than gained through financial riches.

One kind of riches, however, can indeed offer happiness, even though it has nothing to do with earthly wealth. It is God's gift of new life in Christ; a gift not restricted to the few, nor granted through a lottery, but open to all, simply waiting for us to claim it. The more we know and love Jesus, the more we will recognise him as our truest friend, and so discover the wholeness, sense of worth, purpose, rest for our souls and inner contentment that only he can bring. Here is treasure indeed; the one kind of riches that guarantees lasting happiness, now and for all eternity.

Prayer

Loving God,
  for your great gift of life,
  and, above all, for the life you have given me in Christ,
  receive my praise.
Teach me to celebrate all you have given
  and to trust in all you have yet to give,
  through Jesus Christ my Lord.
Amen.

Matthew 6:25-33
The lilies of the field

So, then, I tell you straight, do not vex yourself about life, what you will eat or drink, and do not worry about what you might clothe yourself with. Is not life more than food, and the body more than clothing? Observe the birds flying about you; they do not sow, harvest or hoard reserves in barns, but your heavenly Father feeds them. Are you not much more valuable than they? Which of you by brooding can extend your lifespan by even one hour? So, then, why do you fret over the outfits you're going to wear? See how the wild flowers grow; pay heed to them. They do not labour or weave, yet I can assure you that not even Solomon in all his grandeur was decked out like one of these. If God clothes the grass of the field like this – grass that though here today tomorrow will be tossed on to a bonfire – will he not clothe you all the more richly, you of such little faith? So then, no more of this worrying, these plaintive cries of 'what shall I eat . . . what can I drink . . . what can I wear?' Gentiles crave such things as these; your Father in heaven is well aware of what you need. But seek first the kingdom and righteousness of God, and you will be given everything else you need in addition.

Reflection

'Two men looked out through prison bars; one saw mud, the other saw stars.' I love that old saying. Where one sees ugliness another sees beauty, what brings despair to the first bringing hope to the second. That's not to say everything is subjective; it's rather that on occasions our eyes need to be opened to hidden depths before we can appreciate them.

That, in a sense, is what Jesus was saying in those well-loved words above: look properly at the ordinary things around us, the seemingly mundane things of the natural world, and you will see God's hand behind them. We must beware, of course, of idealising nature too much, for it has its ugly as well as its beautiful side, much of it red in tooth and claw. We are part of an imperfect world in which God's will is as much frustrated as fulfilled, and in which much speaks of the forces of chaos and confusion rather than of order and a loving purpose. Yet, to the eye of faith, there is enough around us, even in things as simple as a flower bursting into bloom or a bird pecking at seed, to speak of the one who lies behind it all: the hand of God that not only fashioned the universe but also reaches out afresh each day providing the essentials of life and the promise of life to come. Despite all that spoils and destroys, denies and disfigures, we can catch sight around us of an architect's design, a creator's power and a sovereign purpose. Let our prayer each day be that God might open our eyes to glimpse a little more clearly these signs of his presence.

Prayer

Creator God,
    I thank you for the world you have made:
    so full of beauty,
    so touched with wonder.
I praise you for its ability to move, astound and refresh,
    and, above all, for the way it speaks
    of your love and purpose.
Forgive me for sometimes losing sight
    of those deeper realities,
    failing to look beneath the surface.
Open my eyes afresh,
    and help me to see your hand in creation
    and your love in the daily routine of life.
In Christ's name I pray.
Amen.

Matthew 7:24-27
Wise and foolish builders

Reading

'Whoever hears my words and acts on them,' said Jesus, 'will be like someone who wisely constructed a house on an outcrop of rock. When the rain poured down, the floodwaters rose and gales battered that house, but it did not collapse, because its foundations were on rock. On the other hand, to hear my words and fail to apply them is akin to the fool who built his house on sand. When this time the rain poured down, the floodwaters rose and gales battered that house, it collapsed – and what a mighty crash it was!'

Reflection

Some time back, I watched a series of television pro-grammes called *Heartbreak Homes*. Among the properties featured were a number along the Norfolk coast; homes that look idyllic yet, in reality, are under sentence, the sea inexorably eating its way into the cliffs towards them. It isn't just a matter of a few inches every decade or so, but rather of several feet every few months, so much so that numerous houses have toppled over the edge within the last few years. The former occupants were understand-ably distraught, having had little inkling of the rate of erosion when they had first moved in. Global warming, coupled with new sea defences further up the coast, have exacerbated what previously had been considered an essentially long-term problem. The foundations of these homes had looked secure enough but they had been ruthlessly exposed.

Reading the familiar parable of Jesus concerning the wise and foolish builders, we may feel it goes without question that we are those who have built on rock, but the above experiences counsel caution. Remember that Jesus didn't just say, 'Everyone who hears my words will be like a wise person who built his house on rock', but, 'Everyone who hears my words *and acts on them*'. The two are very different. It's not hearing the words of Jesus that matters, not even accepting they are true; what counts is whether they make a difference to who we are, whether they change the way we live. Are we still so sure we've built our house on rock?

Prayer

Lord Jesus Christ,
    forgive me, despite your guidance,
    for building my life on sand rather than rock.
Open my ears, my mind and my heart,
    so that I may not only hear what you would say to me
    but also respond with body, mind and soul,
    to the glory of your name.
Amen.

Mark 4:2-9

Sowing the seed

Jesus told the crowd many parables, including this one:
'A farmer went out to sow and, as he did so, some seed
fell by the wayside, and the birds swooped down and
devoured it. Other seed fell on rocky ground, where
there was little soil and, though it sprang up quickly
because the earth was so shallow, when the sun rose it
was baked and withered away, since it had no root. Other
seed fell among thorns, which, as they grew, choked the
seedlings, so that they yielded no grain. Other seed fell
into good soil and brought forth grain, rising up, increas-
ing and yielding thirty-, sixty- and a hundredfold.' And
he said, 'Let those with ears to hear, listen!'

Reflection

What's the most important lesson to be drawn from the
parable of the sower? Is it that our lives need to be like
fertile soil, receptive to the word of God, so that we bear
a rich harvest to his glory? It could be, for there's no
doubt God wants to see that in our lives. Is a more important message that we need to beware of temptations that
may insidiously destroy our faith before we realise what
is happening? It could be that, too, for there's no denying
how real and dangerous temptation can be. Could it be
that the underlying theme is to guard against shallow
discipleship, a faith rooted in a superficial and emotional
response rather than grounded in body, mind and soul?
That's certainly an important point, for how many people
commit themselves to Christ for a moment in a surge of
enthusiasm, only swiftly to fall away? We can even argue

that Jesus is telling us that some people will never respond to the gospel no matter how often they hear it. True perhaps, though it would be foolish to judge the state of another's soul. The truth, of course, is that all of these points are equally valid.

Yet there is a further lesson in these words of Jesus which is, perhaps, more important than any, and that, quite simply, is the need to sow. The seed may be the object of the story, but the sower has first to sow it, and for 'sower' read 'us'. We are the ones called to spread God's word, the responsibility of proclaiming the good news of Christ entrusted to ordinary people like you and me. We cannot guarantee the results of our efforts but one thing is certain: unless we sow the seed, whatever the ground, there will be no harvest.

Prayer

Lord Jesus Christ,
    you have called me to proclaim your name
    and make known your love.
Help me to do that faithfully,
    conscious of my privilege and responsibility.
Teach me to play my part in sowing the seed of your word,
    so that in your own time
    you might bring forth a rich harvest.
In your name I ask it.
Amen.

Faith and doubt

The moment they saw him, the assembled throng could not contain their wonder, and they surged forward to welcome him. 'What were you arguing about?' Jesus asked the disciples. One of the crowd answered him: 'Teacher, I brought my son to see you. A spirit seems to take hold of him, rendering him incapable of speech. It takes hold of him and throws him to the floor, leaving him lying rigid, foaming at the mouth and gnashing his teeth. I implored your disciples to banish it, but it proved beyond them.' 'You faithless bunch!' retorted Jesus. 'Do I have to stay among you for ever? How much longer must I endure this? Bring him to me.' They brought the child to him. Seeing Jesus, the spirit immediately convulsed the boy, and he fell to the ground, rolling about and foaming at the mouth. Jesus asked the father, 'How long has this been happening to him?' 'From infancy,' he answered. 'Many times it has hurled him into flames or water, to destroy him, so if there is anything you can do, for pity's sake help us.' Jesus said to him, 'The question is, can you do anything? All things are possible for the one who believes.' And immediately the father of the child cried out, 'I do believe; help me overcome my unbelief!'

Reflection

'I do believe; help me overcome my unbelief!' How often have we echoed those words? They illustrate the truth that faith often coexists with doubt, the one the flipside of the other. Like the father of the epileptic boy, our hearts say one thing but our minds another. We believe God is love, for example, but occasionally circumstances cause us to question it. We believe he can transform even the worst of situations, but does that include the one we're in now? Sometimes we can't quite suppress those niggling doubts that prevent faith from being as real and vibrant as we want it to be.

For the father in our story, such doubts and questions could all too easily have been the end of the story, but they weren't, because instead of dwelling upon them he was ready to take the leap of faith, responding to Jesus despite them. That's how we too must learn to live with our questions. Our faith does not rest on any collection of creeds, doctrinal statements or set of beliefs but in a personal experience of God in Christ made known through his Spirit. We come to know him not through proving his existence or debating his nature but through responding to his love and committing ourselves to an ongoing relationship. Certainly we must face our questions honestly and openly, but not to the exclusion of all else. Sometimes we have to step out despite them. Instead of dwelling on what we don't know, we need to focus on *who* we do, for what may seem impossible to us, defying all logic and reason, may be perfectly possible for him. Through Christ, offer both your faith and your doubts to God, for however weak the first or strong the second, he is able to work in ways beyond anything you might imagine.

Prayer

Lord,
I want to believe,
but I don't find it easy sometimes,
for there is much I cannot make sense of.
Take both my faith and my doubt,
my certainty and my questions,
and use all to draw me closer to you,
through Jesus Christ my Lord.
Amen.

Mark 14:3-6
An affair of the heart

During his time at Bethany, while he was dining at the house of Simon the leper, a woman came in carrying an alabaster jar of expensive ointment of nard, and, breaking open the jar, she poured the ointment on his head. Some there muttered angrily to each other, 'Why has she wasted the ointment like that? Such ointment could have been sold for over three hundred denarii, and the proceeds given to the poor.' And they reprimanded her. But Jesus said, 'Leave her be; why are you criticising her? She has done a wonderful thing for me.'

Reflection

How far should we allow our hearts to rule our heads? Not at all, you might well say, and, generally, you'd be right. Yet are there not occasions when we need to act on impulse? While it pays to look before we leap, it would be a sad business indeed if we felt it necessary to analyse the pros and cons of every action before ever doing anything. The impulsive gesture can be our undoing, but equally it can be the road to happiness, bringing joy to others and fulfilment to ourselves.

When it comes to relationships, this is all the more so. When we love someone, we want to show it. So it was for the woman who anointed Jesus' feet. She loved Jesus, not in the sense of being physically attracted to him but because of who he was and what he did. She recognised he was someone special, offering a new dimension to life, and instinctively she responded. Do we still have that inner urge to show how much Jesus means to us? Do we find ourselves spontaneously offering our love, our lives, our money, our service? Is our faith still an affair of the heart?

Prayer

Lord Jesus Christ,
    I can never repay all I owe you,
    nor even a fraction of what I have received
    from your loving hand,
    but I yearn to make some kind of response,
    for you have poured out your blessings upon me,
    day after day filling my life with good things.
Receive my worship, my faith and my love,
    for I bring them to you as a small but simple way
    of saying thank you.
Amen.

The Good Samaritan

Anxious to save face, the lawyer asked Jesus, 'Ah yes, but just who is my neighbour?' 'A man was travelling on the Jerusalem–Jericho road,' answered Jesus, 'when he was ambushed by bandits, who beat him up and made off with all he had, even his clothes, leaving him critically ill. A little later, a priest happened to be passing that way. When he saw the unfortunate fellow, he gave him a wide berth and hurried on past. Similarly, a Levite chanced upon him, he too keeping at a safe distance and moving hastily on his way. A Samaritan came by next, and the moment he spotted the man he rushed to his aid. Deeply concerned at his plight, he tended his injuries, salving them with oil and wine. Then, placing the man on his donkey, he took him to an inn and continued to look after him for the rest of the day. Next morning, he handed the innkeeper two coins, with the instruction, "Take good care of him. I'll settle the bill when I return, so don't worry about the cost." What do you reckon: which of these three proved to be a neighbour to the man set upon by bandits?' 'The one who had compassion on him,' answered the lawyer. 'Then off you go and do the same,' said Jesus.

Reflection

'It's a small world', we sometimes say. Today that seems truer than it's ever been. We can travel across the globe in a matter of hours, watch events live by satellite from thousands of miles away, and talk to people in distant continents almost as if they are in our own front room.

That fact brings enormous blessings but also new responsibilities and demands. 'Who is my neighbour?' the lawyer asked Jesus. The answer was anyone and everyone.

Two thousand years ago that challenge must have seemed daunting enough; today it is massive, for suddenly every person in every country has become our concern; every disaster, our disaster; everyone, our neighbour. When floods strike Bangladesh, we know; when famine hits Sudan, we know; when students are massacred in Tiananmen Square, we know. Day after day we are confronted by pictures of emaciated children as we sit down to our meal of plenty; of the homeless as we sit in the warmth and comfort of our homes; of the poor as we enjoy an ever-rising standard of living. All these are our neighbours in today's small world. Charity may begin at home but it cannot end there. By ourselves, of course, we cannot put all the world's ills to right, nor respond to every place of need, but neither can we turn our backs and pretend that they are none of our business. 'Which of these,' said Jesus, 'proved to be a neighbour to the man?' 'The one who had compassion on him,' came the answer. 'Then off you go and do the same!'

Prayer

Living God,
    teach me that this small world is also your world,
    and show me where in responding to others
    I can respond to you.
Amen.

Martha and Mary

As they continued on their way, he entered a certain village, where a woman called Martha welcomed him into her home. She had a sister called Mary, who sat at the Lord's feet, listening to his words. Martha, however, was preoccupied with her many tasks; so she came to him and asked, 'Lord, doesn't it matter to you that my sister has left me to do all the work by myself? Tell her, then, to lend a hand.' But the Lord answered her, 'Martha, Martha, you are fretting and distracted by many things; only one thing is really important. Mary has chosen that more important thing, and it will not be taken away from her.'

Reflection

Stress, we are sometimes told, is a modern-day condition, a product of our high-tech, high-speed age. Certainly, it may be more prevalent today than it once was, but, as the story of Martha and Mary reminds us, it is actually nothing new. At first sight, Martha appears every inch the efficient and competent hostess, unflustered by the unexpected call on her hospitality, but, as her sudden outburst makes plain, inside she feels very different. It's hard not to feel sorry for her, isn't it? If Mary had helped even a little, then the two could have sat down to listen to Jesus together. But would that actually have happened? As I read it, the implication of this story is that Martha would somehow have found something to busy herself with, come what may.

This is a wonderfully human story, but also hugely profound. On one level, it concerns our spiritual well-being.

Don't let your time become so cluttered, says Jesus, that God is squeezed out of it. Don't be so preoccupied with day-to-day pressures, responsibilities and concerns that you neglect the spiritual dimension to life. That warning applies not simply to spiritual matters, but also to life in general. How often do we, like Martha, brood, fret and worry unnecessarily, getting steamed up over things that, in the final analysis, are neither here nor there? To find time to sort out our priorities and focus on what really matters is not easy, but it is essential. Maybe we need more time for our children or partner; perhaps for a friend, neighbour or colleague; or perhaps for ourselves. Perhaps we need to pause and take stock, to consider where we're going and why. Perhaps we need to adapt our lifestyle, modify our ambitions or simply count our blessings. Whatever it is, we do well to make time for the things that really count before the opportunity passes us by.

Prayer

Lord Jesus Christ,
    forgive me for filling my days with frantic activity,
    brooding and worrying over what I cannot change,
    magnifying little things out of all proportion.
Forgive me amid all my daily activity for forgetting to
    make time for you.
Teach me to put you above all else,
    so that I may focus on what really matters
    and know your peace deep within.
Amen.

Luke 15:18-24

The lost son

'I will get up and go to my father,' thought the son, 'and I will say to him, "Father, I have sinned against heaven and before you; I no longer deserve to be called your son; regard me instead as one of your hired hands."' He started back towards his father's house, but as he made his way his father spotted him in the distance and, overcome with emotion, rushed to embrace and kiss him. 'Father,' said the son, 'I've failed both you and God, so I don't deserve to be called your son.' The father, however, ordered his servants, 'Hurry, fetch a robe – the best one – and put it on him; place a ring on his finger and shoes on his feet. Kill the fatted calf and let's have a feast to rejoice; for my son was dead and has been brought back to life; I lost him, but now he's found!'

Reflection

Have you ever sat in a waiting room, wondering when you will be seen to? It's all too common, isn't it, as anyone who has sat in a hospital casualty department or DSS office will know only too well. How much longer will I have to wait? Is there some problem? Will I be seen at all? Such questions inevitably cross one's mind. Even worse, though, is sitting as a child outside the head teacher's office, waiting to be summoned after committing some misdemeanour – not that I would know, of course! What sort of reception is likely there? What kind of punishment lies in store?

Some people approach God like that, wondering whether he will receive them and afraid of the consequences if he does. 'Can he truly have time for someone like me?' they ask themselves. 'Of course not! Can he possibly forgive my many mistakes? It beggars belief.' If that's how you feel, then look again at the parable of the lost son, for there we see one of the most memorable pictures of God in the whole Bible; a God who waits to greet us while we are still far off, reaching out to embrace us in love. With him, there is no question of being kept outside, left to stew and finally made to suffer. On the contrary, we need only make the first tentative steps of approach and he is there waiting to receive us, longing to welcome us home.

Prayer

Loving God,
    remind me that, however often I might go astray,
    your love goes on seeking me out.
Remind me that you are always ready
    to forgive and forget,
    to put the past behind me
    and to welcome me back.
In Christ's name I thank you.
Amen.

Luke 21:1-4
The widow's offering

Looking up, he saw well-to-do people putting their gifts into the treasury, and, alongside them, a poor widow offering two small copper coins. 'Mark my words,' he said, 'this poor widow has put in more than all of the others; for they have contributed out of their plenty, but she, despite her poverty, has put in everything she had to live on.'

Reflection

'And now the collection will be received.' Whenever I hear words like those in the context of worship they make me wince, for they convey an idea that reinforces a fundamental misunderstanding of what Christian giving is all about. The implication is that we give out of duty: not because we may but because we must, because it is expected of us. What a contrast between that and the widow at the treasury. Humanly speaking, her gift was pathetic, barely worth the bother of counting it, but as far as God was concerned it was a priceless treasure, because it was given not as a collection but as an offering. She gave it because she wanted to, because she was eager to respond, and she gave sacrificially because she wanted to tell God how much he meant to her.

We can apply her example not only to the giving of our money but also of our time, our prayers, our love and our service. Do we truly *offer* those to God, or do we give them mechanically, half-heartedly, grudgingly? Do we bring them out of routine or habit, or as a spontaneous expression of love and thanksgiving? 'It's the thought that counts,' we are often told. In terms of our response to God, those are words well worth pondering.

Prayer

Loving God,
    you gave without counting the cost,
    your sole desire to share your love and impart your joy.
Help me to give back to you in return,
    not as a duty or an afterthought,
    but as a joyful privilege,
    a giving of my best,
    an offering from the heart.
Take what I am
    and consecrate it to your service,
    in the name of Christ.
Amen.

John 3:16
God so loved the world

God so loved the world that he offered his only Son, so that all those who believe in him need not die but may receive eternal life.

Reflection

'I believe in God, the Father almighty, maker of heaven and earth.' So say the opening words of the Apostle's Creed, a statement of faith designed to encapsulate the essential convictions of Christian belief; to summarise what we believe, or, at least, what we are meant to believe. Yet, all such creeds leave one thing out: a statement that, for me, is more important than any other; namely, the affirmation that God believes in us! We are talking, of course, about a different kind of belief, though it is not as different as you might at first think. What we see in the birth of Jesus is God firmly and resoundingly declaring, 'I believe in humankind!'

To understand the full wonder behind that statement we need to remind ourselves of what, in the biblical sense, it means to say, 'I believe'. It doesn't mean accepting the existence of something, in the sense that we might believe in ghosts or flying saucers. It means belief in the sense of trust, putting one's faith in something, and being ready, if necessary, to stake one's name and reputation on the object of that belief. Seen in this light, how many people do we truly believe in? Yet, that is the belief God has in us. He doesn't see us through rose-coloured spectacles. He is not blind for a moment to our fallibility and sinfulness. Yet, despite all that is wrong in our lives, he sees something precious in us, special and worth saving – even worth dying for! In the stable in Bethlehem, the child in a manger, and the life, death and resurrection that followed, we see God's emphatic 'yes' to humankind, his affirmation of our worth! The creeds are important, don't get me wrong, but they don't quite say everything, for it seems to me that if we haven't understood that God believes in us, we haven't really understood what it means to say, 'I believe in God'.

Prayer
Gracious God,
    help me to believe in you
    as much as you believe in me.
Amen.

John 8:31b-32

The truth that sets us free

If you continue in my word, and truly live as my disciples, then you will know the truth and the truth will set you free.

Reflection

What implements would you need if you were held captive somewhere and attempting to escape? A file or hacksaw perhaps, to cut through the bars of your prison, or possibly a crowbar to force them apart? Better still, a skeleton key so that you could open the door and walk away? One resource that wouldn't immediately spring to mind is that which Jesus offers his followers: truth. What good could that be in making a bid for freedom? In terms of physical captivity, the answer, of course, is precious little, but the imprisonment and freedom Jesus has in mind is very different. It relates to the need for an inner liberation, a release from all that holds us captive and prevents us from living life to the full. In other words, it concerns setting us free from whatever alienates us from ourselves, from one another and from God.

Across the years people have searched for such free-dom, even though many would not be able to put into words exactly what they are looking for. Some seek the answer in money and possessions, others in sex and drugs, others again in a hobby, relationship, cult or phil-osophy, and so we could go on. For all our modern-day prosperity and sophistication, we are still aware of an inner void, a thirst for something of ultimate value and meaning. According to St Augustine, that thirst – recog-nised or unrecognised – is for God. 'You stir our hearts,' he wrote, 'to delight in praising you, because you have made us restless for yourself, and our hearts are restless until they find their rest in you.' If that, though, represents the diagnosis, in the words of Jesus we find the cure. In him we discover truth – not some abstract concept but the truth about life and about God, a glimpse into the heartbeat of the universe. From him we receive unconditional acceptance – an acceptance that gives us the sense of purpose and fulfilment that otherwise seems to elude us. Through him we find freedom to live life to the full, both now and for all eternity.

Prayer

Merciful God,
 teach me to trust in your love
 and rejoice in your mercy.
Help me to let go of the recriminations, doubt and fears
 that hold me captive
 and to accept the freedom
 you have won for me in Christ.
Grant that I might not simply talk about new life
 but live it joyfully,
 receiving it each moment as your gracious gift,
 in the name of Christ.
Amen.

John 10:10

You shall!

I have come so that you shall have life, and have it to the full.

Reflection

'Don't do that!' 'Stop it!' 'Leave it alone!' There are times when being a parent feels like constantly nagging, forever saying no. The same, sadly, is the impression some people have of the Church; a view reinforced by those old Wayside Pulpit posters you still sometimes see, starkly proclaiming 'The wages of sin is death' or some other equally cheery message! Undeniably, there is a negative element in the Bible, epitomised by the majority of the Ten Commandments with their stern preface 'Thou shalt not . . .'

This, however, is by no means the whole story, for in the teaching of Jesus the message is reversed. Instead of 'You shall not' it becomes 'You shall', all the negative commandments being summed up in one positive injunction, encapsulated in that promise of Jesus: 'you shall have life, and have it to the full'. Repeatedly it is the same story: 'ask and you will receive, seek and you will find, knock and the door will be opened to you' – the blind shall see, the lame walk, the imprisoned be set free, the pure in heart see God, the hungry and thirsty be satisfied, and so on and so on. Never think that being a Christian is about what you *can't* do, still less give that impression to others. Above all, it is about what you *can* do; about the possibilities the love of Christ opens up; about the sheer potential of life lived with him!

Prayer

Generous and life-giving God,
  I thank you that you came in Christ
  not to exact punishment but to show mercy;
  not to restrict but to liberate,
  not to deny but to affirm.
Forgive me for sometimes turning joyful faith
  into sombre religion,
  the living gospel into lifeless dogma,
  a message of hope into a foretelling of doom.
Teach me to receive the gifts you want me to enjoy
  and to turn life into a celebration of your goodness,
  so that the person I am,
  as well as the words I say,
  may truly proclaim the good news of Jesus Christ.
Amen.

A peace that passes understanding

'My legacy to you is peace,' said Jesus. 'That's what I give you: my very own peace, unlike anything the world can offer. Don't let anything disturb or distress you. Put your mind at rest and fear nothing.'

Reflection

A common marketing ploy today seems to be to promise peace of mind. Take out a pension plan or an insurance policy and you can put your worries behind you. Go on holiday to the sun and get away from it all. Buy a new car, washing machine or stereo system and take the hassle out of life. Anything and everything, it seems, promises us a more relaxed and happy existence. Sadly, however, statistics don't bear this out. We may have more leisure time and money today than previous generations, and we may enjoy all the latest hi-tech gadgetry, yet we live in a world where stress is rife and where countless people yearn for a sense of inner peace. Peace, like happiness, cannot be bought; indeed, the quest for money, possessions and status is often what destroys the little peace we have.

We can find a degree of peace in this world in the sense of briefly getting away from it all, but for the Christian real peace comes ultimately from another source – from an awareness of God's love made real through the inner presence of his Holy Spirit. We cannot create such peace ourselves, but we can cultivate it through making time for God, creating a space in our lives for prayer and reflection, and being open to what he would do within us. Such peace involves letting go and seeing life from another perspective than that typically adopted, but it also means taking hold of a prize greater than anything the world can give – a peace that passes understanding.

Prayer

Loving God,
    wherever I am,
    wherever I go,
    whatever I do,
    however I feel,
    I know that you will be with me,
    to hold,
    to heal,
    to guide
    and to bless.
So, I will go in peace,
    assured of your unfailing love.
Amen.